SWEAR LIKE DADDY

Summersdale Publishers Ltd
46 West Street
Chichester
West Sussex
PO19 1RP
UK

www.summersdale.com

Printed and bound in China

ISBN: 978-1-84953-469-7

Substantial discounts on bulk quantities of Summersdale books are available to corporations, professional associations and other organisations. For details contact Nicky Douglas by telephone: +44 (0) 1243 756902, fax: +44 (0) 1243 786300 or email: nicky@summersdale.com.

SWEAR LiKE DADDY

by darren cezanne

Introduction

Every Daddy knows he leads by example and acts accordingly, forcing vegetables down at mealtimes and always saying 'please' and 'thank you'. But even the best-behaved Daddies can f*ck up! Every Daddy has those moments when he forgets who might be listening as he turns the air blue, only to discover later his little copycat darling repeating their new bestest 'Daddy word'. This colourful compendium captures some of those magical moments for the whole family to cherish.

B is for bollocks

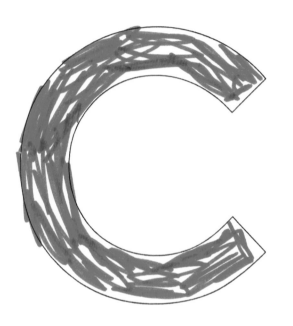

F is for fuck fuckface fucker>

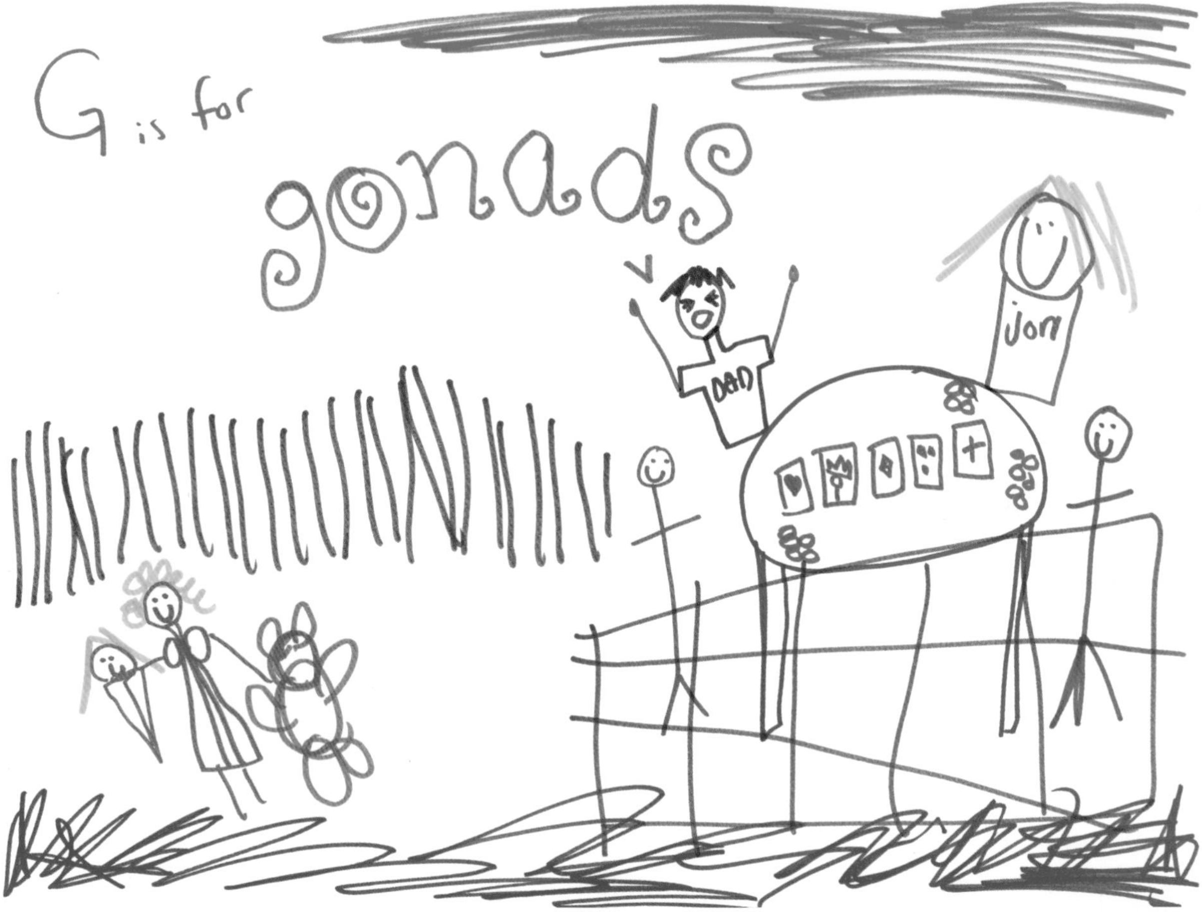
G is for
gonads
DAD
Jon

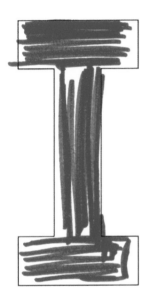

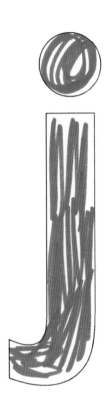

J is for

jugs + jubblies

K is for Knackers

N is for nobhead

 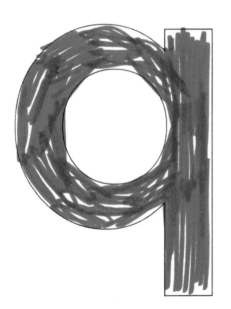

Q is for QUIM

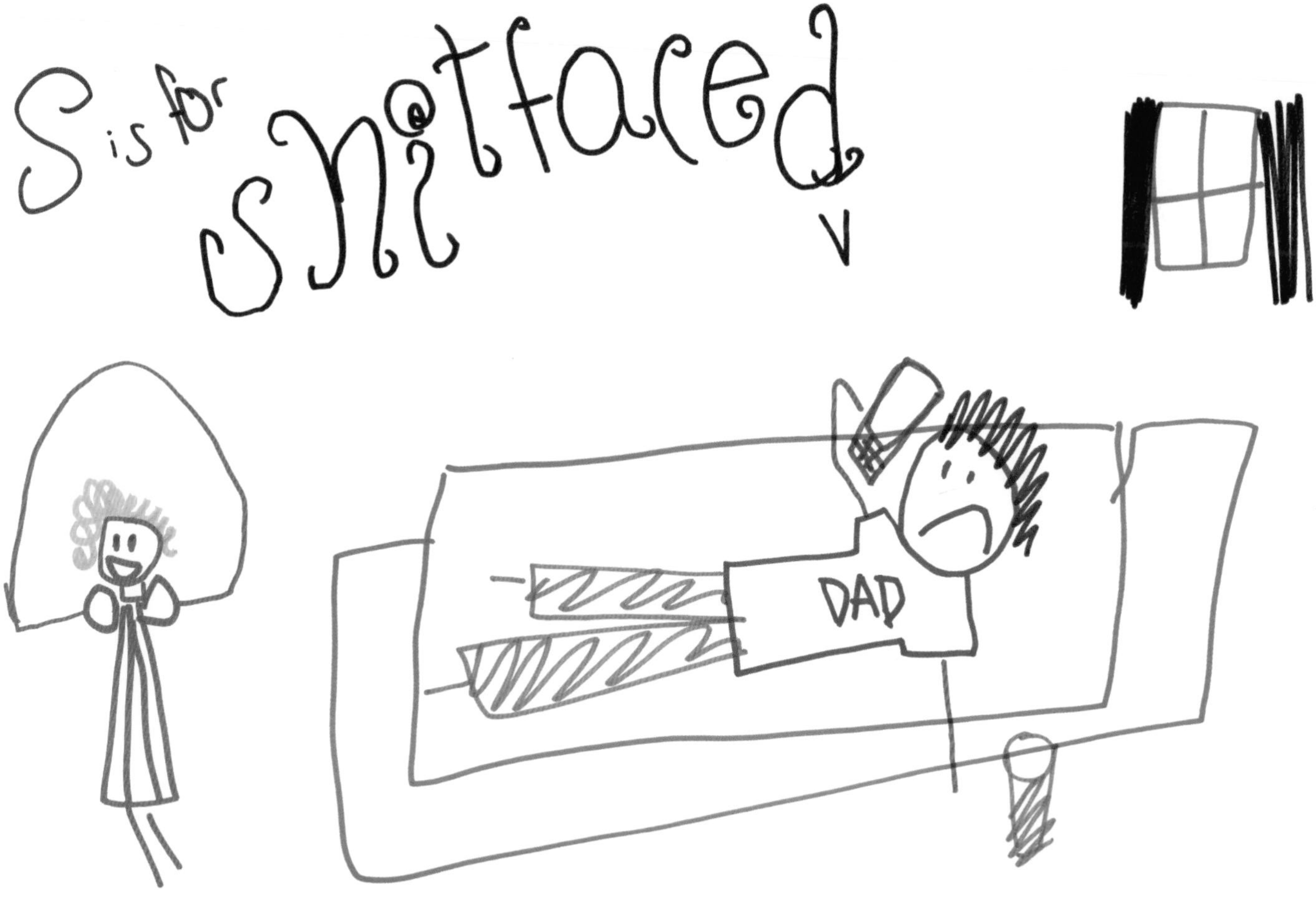
S is for shitfaced
DAD

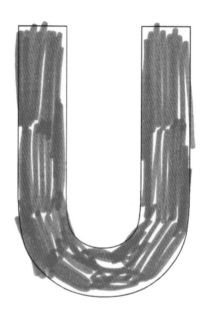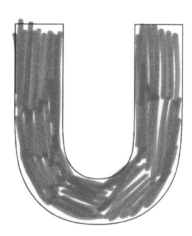

U is for ugly fat fuck

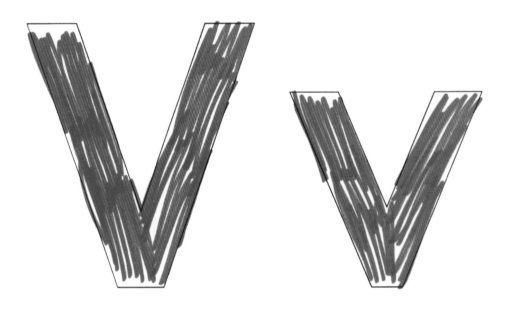

X is for XXX sluts

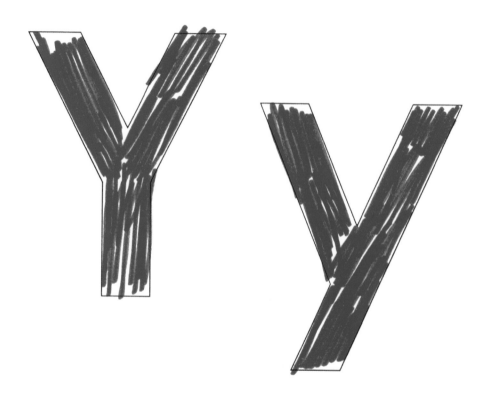

Words I've Learnt...

Aa..

....

Bb..

....

Cc..

....

Dd..

....

Ee..

....

Ff..

....

Gg..

....

Hh..

....

Ii..

....

Jj..

....

Kk..

....

Ll...
....

Mm..
....

Nn...
....

Oo...
....

Pp...
....

Qq...
....

Rr..

....

Ss..

....

Tt..

....

Uu..

....

Vv..

....

Ww..

....

Xx..
....

Yy..
....

Zz..
....

If you're interested in finding out more about
our books, find us on Facebook at
Summersdale Publishers
and follow us on Twitter at
@Summersdale.

www.summersdale.com